CONTENTS

About the Authors

Authors Josh and Sean McDowell collaborated with their writer to bring you this Unshakable Truth Journey course. The content is based upon Scripture and the McDowells' book *The Unshakable Truth*.®

Over 45-plus years, **Josh McDowell** has spoken to more than 10 million people in 120 countries about the evidence for Christianity and the difference the Christian faith makes in the world. He has authored or coauthored more than 120 books (with more than 51 million copies in print), including such classics as *More Than a Carpenter* and *New Evidence That Demands a Verdict*.

Sean McDowell is an educator and a popular speaker at schools, churches, and conferences nationwide. He is author of *Ethix: Being Bold in a Whatever World*, coauthor of *Understanding Intelligent Design*, and general editor of *Apologetics for a New Generation* and *The Apologetics Study Bible for Students*. He is currently pursuing a PhD in apologetics and worldview studies. Sean's website, www.seanmcdowell.org, offers his blog, many articles and videos, and much additional curriculum.

About the Writer

Dave Bellis is a ministry consultant focusing on ministry planning and product development. He is a writer, producer, and product developer. He and his wife, Becky, have two grown children and live in northeastern Ohio.

Acknowledgments

We would like to thank the many people who brought creativity and insight to forming this course:

Terri Snead and David Ferguson of Great Commandment Network for their writing insights for the TruthTalk and Truth Encounter sections of this study guide.

Terry Glaspey for his insights and guidance as he helped in the development of the Unshakable Truth Journey concept.

Paul Gossard for his skillful editing of this manuscript.

And finally, the entire team at Harvest House, who graciously endured the process with us.

Josh McDowell
Sean McDowell
Dave Bellis

What Is the Unshakable Truth Journey All About?

You hear people talk about having a personal relationship with God and knowing Christ. But what does that really mean? Sure, they probably are saying they are a Christian and God has personally forgiven them of their sins. But is that all of what being a Christian really is—being a person forgiven by God?

We are here to say that being a follower of Christ is much, much more than that. Everything you are and what you are becoming as a person is wrapped up in it. When Jesus said he was "the way, the truth, and the life" (John 14:6) he was offering us a supernatural way to follow in his way, his truth, and his life. As we do, we begin to understand what we were meant to know

and be and how we were meant to live. Actually, when we become a follower of Christ we begin to take on Jesus' view of the world and begin to think like and be motivated like and live like Christ. And that brings incredible joy and satisfaction to life.

So when we see life and relationships as Jesus sees them, we begin to get a clear picture of who we are and discover our true identity. We begin to realize why we are here and recognize our purpose and meaning in life. We begin to know where we are going and experience our destiny and mission in a life larger than ourselves. Being a Christian—a committed follower of Christ—unlocks our identity, purpose, and destiny in life. It is then that the natural process of spiritual reproduction takes place. That is when imparting the faith to our family and others around us becomes a reality. But what is involved in being that kind of a follower of Christ—a person who has joy and satisfaction in life and knows how to effectively impart the faith to the next generation?

The Unshakable Truth Journey gets to the core of what being a true follower of Christ means and what knowing Christ is all about. Together you and your group will begin a journey that will last a lifetime. It is a journey into what you as a follower of Christ are to believe biblically, how you process your beliefs into core values, and how you live them out in all your relationships. In fact, we will take the core truths of Christianity and break them down into a five-step process:

1. ***What truths do you as a Christian believe biblically?***

    In the first step you and your group will interact
    with what we as Christians believe about God,
    his Word, and so on.

2. ***Why do you believe those truths?***

    Sure, you can say you believe certain truths
    because they are biblical, but when you know
    why they are true it grounds you in your faith.
    Additionally, it gives you confidence to pass
    them on to others—especially your family.

3. ***How are these truths relevant to life?***

    In many respects truth isn't very meaningful
    until you see how it is relevant to your own life.

4. ***How do you live these truths out personally?***

    Knowing how the truth of Christianity is relevant
    is necessary, but what it leads to is understand-
    ing how that truth is to become a living reality in
    your own life. That's where the rubber meets the
    road, so to speak.

5. ***How do you, as a group, live these truths out
    before your community and world?***

    As Christians we are all to be "salt" and "light" to

the world around us. In this step you and your group will discover how to impact your own community with truth that is lived out corporately—as a body.

Be warned! The Unshakable Truth Journey isn't a program to study what Christianity is all about. Simply discovering what something is about has great limitations and ends up being of little value. Rather, this journey is about experiencing firsthand how God's truth is to be experienced in your life right now and, in fact, for the rest of your life. It's is about knowing God's truth in a real, experiential way. The apostle John said, "It is by our actions that we know we are living in the truth" (1 John 3:19). You will be challenged repeatedly to increasingly know certain truths by experiencing them continually in your relationship with God and with those around you. It is then you will be able to pass on this ever-increasing faith journey to your family and friends.

There will be two specific exercises that appear throughout these courses. The first is entitled "Truth Encounter." This section is an invitation for you to stop and carefully reflect on the truth of each session. You'll be asked to encounter a truth of God as you relate personally with Jesus, as you live out the truth of God's Word with your small group, or as you relate personally with his people. Please don't rush past these Truth Encounters. They are designed to equip you in how to experience truth right in the room you're in!

The second exercise is an assignment for the week, called "TruthTalk." The TruthTalks are designed as conversation starters—ways to engage others in spiritual discussions. They will create opportunities for you to share what you've experienced in this course with others around you. This will help you communicate God's truth with others as you share vulnerably about your own Unshakable Truth Journey.

What you discover here is to last a lifetime and beyond because God's truths are designed to be enjoyed forever. You see, experiencing God's truth and knowing him will grow throughout eternity, and your love of him will expand to contain it. And that process begins in the here and now. Your relationship with God may have begun 5 months, 5 years, or 50 years ago—it doesn't matter. The truths explored in these courses are to be applied at every level of life. And what is so encouraging is that while these truths are eternally deep they can be embraced and experienced by even a young child. That is the beauty and mystery of God's truth!

This particular Unshakable Truth Journey is one of 12 different growth guides. All the growth guides are based upon Josh and Sean McDowell's book *The Unshakable Truth*, which is the companion book to this course. The book covers 12 core truths of the Christian faith. The growth guide you have in your hand covers the truth about original sin and how to make right choices. Together we will explore our problem with sin and the

value God places on us in spite of our sin. These five sessions lay the foundation for how to make right choices in life. Check out the other Unshakable Truth Journey courses in the appendix of this growth guide.

Okay then, let our journey begin.

WHAT WE BELIEVE ABOUT SIN

It seems we as humans try to find excuses for our wrong behavior. What are some odd or "humorous" excuses your children or friends have made in the past when they were caught doing wrong? What was the offense, and what was the excuse?

_____

_____

_____

_____

Someone read Genesis 3:11-13.

Why do we all tend to make excuses when we do wrong?

_____

_____

_____

_____

Someone read Romans 3:9-12.

We have a world with a bent for doing wrong. But at its core, what makes sin, sin? How would you define sin?

_____

_____

_____

_____

OUR GROUP OBJECTIVE

To gain a greater understanding of what sin is and how the first human sin affected the human race, and develop a deeper sense of gratitude for God's response to sin.

Someone read the following aloud. (This is drawn from chapter 12 of *The Unshakable Truth* book.)

> Humans were created in the image of a triune God whose Persons are in perfect, harmonious relationship with one another. He wanted the first couple to join the Godhead's relational union. This perfect circle of loving relationship was God's ultimate intention for all humanity from creation forward.

He intended Adam and Eve and all their descendants to be ecstatically happy in such a loving relationship with him and each other forever. And at first in Eden, it all worked perfectly. But something went terribly wrong.

There is no hint in Scripture that the perfect relationship between humans and God would continue automatically. It was based on an authentic love that was to be expressed freely and voluntarily. Therefore the close relationship involved a choice and was to bear the fruit of trust. Of course, God is all-powerful and could have created humans with no choice capacity at all. He could have manipulated their every move and made them conform to his every wish. But had he done this, they would not have been created in his own image. God is free to choose, and he gave humans that same capacity. Adam and Eve exercised that capacity to choose by joining God's circle of relationship and freely and voluntarily expressing their love to him and one another.

From God's side, the relationship was devoid of any self-serving power plays, desires to control another person, or ambitions of independence. It was a relationship that was other-focused. In it, he chose to look for the best in the other and freely gave of himself to please the other. When a person

knows another and has voluntarily chosen to love him or her this way, it engenders an intimate and trusting relationship.

So, in the pristine perfection of the Garden, God offered Adam and Eve a tangible way of expressing their unselfish love and trust in him. He gave them a command not to eat of a certain fruit. And so there it was: They had a choice to make, a voluntary choice to believe that God was acting unselfishly and had their best interest at heart. Or they could choose to believe that he was selfishly keeping something good from them.

In this simple choice Adam and Eve were being asked to show that they trusted that God was good and would not selfishly withhold things from them. To choose against trust would be to destroy the loving relationship established between them and him. And to sever that relationship would mean becoming unplugged from the only true source of love and life itself. That, of course, is what happened when Adam and Eve chose to disregard God's command.

Let's say you tell a three-year-old child not to cross the street until you give him or her the okay to walk across beside you. If he or she disregards your instructions and darts out before you

say, what in the relationship has been violated? (It is the same relational violation that Adam and Eve committed toward God.)

_____

_____

_____

_____

Someone read Exodus 34:14.

God wants us to obey and worship him exclusively and is jealous if we do not. What is his motive behind getting us to act and live and relate in a godly way—the way he does?

_____

_____

_____

_____

Someone read the following:

> God is love, joy, peace, goodness, and everything
> needed to bring pure happiness and joy. "Whatever
> is good and perfect," James declares, "comes to us
> from God" (James 1:17). So when God told Adam
> and Eve to avoid that fruit, he was actually lead-
> ing them to unselfish, other-focused living in rela-
> tionship with him—the kind of relationship that

would bring great pleasure to him and deep happiness to them.

Do you want to modify the definition of sin that you previously wrote? If so, how?

_____

_____

_____

_____

||||||||||||||||||||||||||||||||||||||||||||||||||||||||||||||||||||||||||||||||||||||||||||||||||||||
The Results of Being
Unplugged from God

Try one of these two experiments:

Experiment #1: Unplug a lamp in the room or flip a light switch off.

Experiment #2: Hold your breath for as long as you can.

Result #1: What happened to the lamp when it was unplugged or when the the light had the flow of current to it broken? _____

_____

_____

Result #2: What happens when your oxygen supply is cut off? _____

_____

_____

A light needs a power source to operate. Our bodies need oxygen. There are consequences if these things are cut off. The same is true if a life is disconnected from God.

Someone read John 1:4.

Take a moment and discuss some of the present and future consequences of the human race being relationally disconnected and alienated from God because of sin. Begin by completing the sentences below.

- Without a relational connection to God, who is the true source of love, humans will experience _____

    _____

    _____.

- Without a relational connection to God, who is the true source of joy, humans will experience _____

    _____

    _____.

- Without a relational connection to God, who is the true source of peace, humans will experience _____

    _____.

Someone read the following.

> The entrance of sin drove life from the world. By sinning, Adam and Eve demonstrated they didn't trust God to have their best interest at heart. Their choice to be self-sovereign and decide for themselves what was right and good for them disrupted their relational connection to a perfect and holy God—who is life itself and from whom all life comes (see John 1:4; 5:26). Gone were the thrills of intimacy and joy shared with their Father God. Gone were the moments of laughter enjoyed together. Gone was their close relationship.
>
> Not only did their sin bring into the world the living death of separation from God, but sin's fallout brought hunger, disease, hatred, and heartache that would end in physical death and eternal separation from God. Sin and death reigned over the whole human race from that moment forward. Scripture states, "When Adam sinned, sin entered the entire human race. Adam's sin brought death, so death spread to everyone, for everyone sinned" (Romans 5:12).

Sin brought death—a relational disconnect and complete relational separation from God. Apart from Christ, what can reverse this disconnect? What can you and I possibly do (again, apart from Christ's plan of salvation) to find favor with God? Describe

how and why people think their own efforts can successfully reconnect them to God. Or describe why such efforts cannot successfully reconnect us to God. Then share your insights with the group.

_____

_____

_____

Someone read the following.

> Most people believe that if our good deeds out-weigh our bad deeds, God will give us credit for our effort and let us into his heaven. The problem is that we are all dead to God because of sin. Good deeds, no matter how many and how high their quality, can't change our status of being dead. Dead people simply have no ability to save themselves— because they are dead.

Someone read Romans 7:21-24.

Seriously, how big an issue is the sin problem? Do you believe the entire race of human beings is truly without hope of gaining favor with God through our own strength? _____

Keeping in mind the reality that sin brought death to the human race, read the following belief statement.

We believe the truth that God created humans in his image to relate to him lovingly, but that relationship was destroyed because of original sin. Sin was passed to the entire human race, and consequently all are born spiritually dead and utterly helpless to gain favor with God.

What does the reality of being "utterly helpless" (Romans 5:6) cause you to feel? Who do you look to for a solution? Where is your hope?

_____

_____

_____

Truth Encounter

Someone read Genesis 3:15.

What was God announcing to us in this verse?

_____

_____

_____

As God addressed the very first sin, he was already declaring Christ's victory over Satan and the effects of sin. As God explained the painful effects of the first sin, he was also announcing his plan for redemption.

The perfect and holy Creator experienced his children being separated from his presence. Because of their choices, Adam and Eve became disconnected from God—the only source that could sustain life, love, joy, and peace. How do you think this made God feel? Someone read Genesis 6:6.

_____

_____

_____

Take a moment to remember the story of the prodigal son in Luke 15. The father's heart was filled with sadness when he was separated from his son. The father hurt over the disconnection between himself and the one he loved. How would you feel if one of your children rejected you and ran away from home?

_____

_____

_____

How does it make you feel to know that God's heart hurts when he thinks about being separated from you?

_____

_____

_____

To what extent and to what lengths did God go to relationally reconnect you to himself? Someone read Romans 5:6.

_____

_____

Your sin nailed Jesus to the cross, yet he loved you enough to die in order to redeem you. What does this prompt you to feel and say?

_____

_____

_____

Someone read the following verse.

"Let all who seek You rejoice and be glad in You; and let those who love Your salvation say continually, 'Let God be magnified'" (Psalm 70:4 NASB).

Take the next few moments and share your heart response to God in a declaration of praise in songs of worship and in prayers of gratitude.

"Let God be magnified because _____

_____

_____."

(For example: "Let God be magnified because he took initiative to come 'looking for me' just like he did for Adam and Eve. I am so grateful for how his heart longs for relationship with me.")

TruthTalk—An Assignment of the Week

Take time this week to share with a family member or friend what you have discovered in this session. Consider saying something like:

There is absolutely nothing we can do on our own to solve our sin problem because we are all dead spiritually and will soon be dead physically…As a result of sin and death, the universe is in a state of entropy—moving from order to disorder. Everything is dying, and no amount of human ingenuity or technology or medical advances can permanently reverse the inevitable doom

1 "I used to believe that if my good deeds outweighed my bad deeds, God would let me slide into heaven. I now know that isn't how it works. Can I tell you what I've learned recently? For example…

_____

_____

_____."

2 "I have always thought of God as one who doesn't want us to sin, just because he told us not to— but I've recently learned that God is much more concerned about my relationship with him. When I disobey God he…

_____

_____

_____."

of us all. That is, nothing apart from a miraculous intervention by God.

3 "Do you remember how you feel sad sometimes when you are separated from Mom/Dad? God feels like that too. He feels sad when we are separated from him by the wrong things we do and say. Our wrong choices are like a big wall that separates us from God. Here's the good news, though…

_____

_____

_____."

Read chapter 12 of *The Unshakable Truth* book as a review of this lesson and chapter 13 for the next session.

EVIDENCE THAT SIN HAS CONSEQUENCES

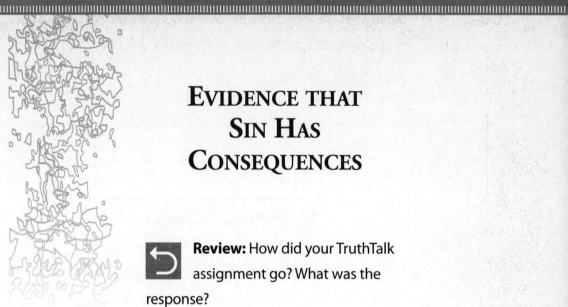

Review: How did your TruthTalk assignment go? What was the response?

_____

_____

_____

_____

Before coming together as a group today you probably read the newspaper, listened to or watched the news, read something online, or heard people talking about events in your community or around the world. Describe two or three things that are going on in the world today that are less than ideal. What are some problems, disagreements, conflicts, killings, and so on that you are aware of?

_____

_____

_____

_____

What is the root of these problems? What is the root cause of all disagreements, conflicts, or troubles that we have in the world?

_____

_____

_____

_____

OUR GROUP OBJECTIVE

To explore the source of sin and examine our own hearts so we can more clearly understand what sin does to us and to God.

Someone read Matthew 15:10-20.

In this passage, what truth is Jesus trying to get his disciples to understand?

_____

_____

_____

_____

So lying, cheating, lust, pride, and other sins come from the heart.

Someone read 1 John 2:15-16.

Based on these verses, a love of the world or a sinful heart craves three things. What are they?

Craving or lust of _____.

Craving or lust of _____.

Craving or lust of _____.

From the sinful heart of fallen humans comes the craving of physical gratification, greed for things a person sees, and arrogant pride in what a person has (possessions) and has done (accomplishments).

Someone read Philippians 2:3-4 and Galatians 5:13-14.

Describe the characteristics of the sinful nature. What drives the lustful desire of physical gratification, greed, and pride in a person's heart?

_____

_____

_____

_____

_____

_____

Someone read the following. (This is drawn from chapter 13 of *The Unshakable Truth* book.)

> Greed, lustful gratification, arrogant pride, distrust, deception, conflicts, murder, war, destruction, and all the evils of this world can be traced back to the human heart bent on satisfying self—self-centeredness and prideful self-reliance.
>
> Lust (sin) desires to selfishly take rather than to give. It is all about serving self regardless of how it affects another. It is a self-centered condition that focuses only on meeting its own needs—it is not other-focused.
>
> Lust (sin) desires to focus on "number one"—to be seen and get credit for what has been accomplished. It boasts and wants to be favored for what it has and what it has done. Instead of being reliant on and recognizing its need for God and others, it chooses to be self-sovereign and pridefully directs its own path to gratify self.
>
> "Mine," "me," "my way" is the attitude of sin. Adam and Eve chose this route. Rather than believing that God was good, and trusting that he had their best interest at heart, they chose a self-centered and prideful, self-reliant course. Rather than walking in God's way, they walked

in their own way. This approach is the opposite of Christ's—he humbled himself even to the point of submitting to death on a cross because of his love for others. The result was the salvation of many.

Sin, on the other hand, focuses on self, and the result is costly for both the selfish and the innocent. The Old Testament has this theme woven throughout. It tells of a people who at times walk in the ways of God. They live out godly relationships and reap the benefits of joy and happiness. Then we learn that they sin—they act self-centered and self-reliant and do not trust in God and his ways. Throughout the history of the nation, this turning away from God accelerates, and in spite of the warnings of several prophets, the people do not repent, and they refuse to turn back to him. Consequently "disaster came upon the nation of Israel because the people worshiped other gods, sinning against the Lord their God, who had brought them safely out of their slavery in Egypt" (2 Kings 17:7). The result is always the same: pain and suffering, heartache and ruin, destruction and death. It is death that ultimately is the wages of sin, just as God declared to Adam and Eve. History records it; we see it all around us; we experience it in our own lives.

Historically, has our nation or have other nations of the world

gone down a prideful, self-reliant, or self-centered path that has brought negative consequences? Describe what some of those self-reliant or self-centered choices have produced within your generation.

_____

_____

_____

_____

_____

_____

_____

Be vulnerable for a moment and think of how self-centeredness or prideful self-reliance plays a role in your life. Do you struggle with self-centeredness? Do you tend to be "me-focused" or "my-way-focused," wanting to be seen as the one accomplishing things? Open your heart to God and ask him to search it.

Someone read Psalm 139:23-24.

Now, pray the prayer of Psalm 139. Your prayers might sound like:

"Search me, God, and know my heart. Test me and reveal the things that ought to worry me about my life; and then lead me in the way that's yours."

Next, take a few moments to ask God to show you yourself and

those areas that are self-focused and unlike him. Then write down what he, the God who loves you for who you are, has shown you. Describe areas in your life that reflect themselves in self-centeredness or prideful self-reliance.

_____

_____

_____

_____

_____

_____

Truth Encounter

Someone read James 5:16.

Now, live out the truth of this Scripture. Confess your sins to each other so that God might bring about healing. Without revealing anything hurtful of another person, in wisdom, confess to others in the group your own struggle with sin—your self-centered or prideful, self-reliant condition.

_____

_____

_____

_____

_____

_____

How does acting out of your sinful nature tend to bring pain, suffering, and heartache to your own life and to those around you?

_____

_____

_____

_____

_____

How do you think God responds personally to your sinful ways?

_____

_____

_____

_____

_____

Reflect again on God's heart response to the sinful world in Noah's time. Someone read Genesis 6:6. Does God's heart break when you sin? Why?

_____

_____

_____

_____

When Jesus was on earth, the people of Israel were rejecting him as their Messiah—their Redeemer. What was the attitude of his heart as the people turned him away? Someone read Matthew 23:37-38.

_____

_____

_____

_____

As a review of last week's session, why do you suppose it saddens the heart of God when we choose to walk in our own ways and reject him and his ways?

_____

_____

_____

_____

Someone read 1 John 1:9.

Just as God was grieved for the people of Noah's day, he is grieved when he sees our sin. It hurts his heart. He is grieved because our sin separates us from him, and that separation hurts all of our relationships. His heart is saddened because he sees how sin hurts us—the ones he loves! And ultimately, his heart is grieved because our sin is why his Son had to die.

However, God is a God who is both rich in mercy and ultimate in holiness. He is so holy that he cannot relate to sin in any

form. So rather than lose relationship with us, he restored the possibility of relationship by sacrificing his Son. How do you feel as you consider the personal connection between your sin and Christ's death?

Complete this sentence:

"As I think about how Christ gave his life for my sin, I feel _____

_____

_____

_____

_____."

Next, take a few moments and express your confession and gratitude to God. Quietly reflect on these truths together with him. If you have identified sins that have separated you from him, tell him. If you have come to sense a new way that you have hurt him or hurt others by your self-centeredness or prideful self-reliance, confess those now. Live out the truth of 1 John 1:9.

Think of this prayer as your own:

"God, I am grateful for your heart toward my sin. I am grateful you have died for me. My self-centeredness and self-reliance have been wrong. My sin has hurt you and hurt others. Please forgive me and wash me clean."

Someone read Psalm 51:7-13.

Pray together as a group and consider singing a song of worship.

_____

_____

_____

Truth Talk—An Assignment of the Week

This week take time to share with a family member or friend what you have been learning about sin. Consider saying something like:

1 "I've come to realize that God's heart hurts when I make wrong choices. That truth has made me love God even more because

_____

_____

_____."

2 "I've been going through a study on what sin does to people,

Each of us has personal examples of the negative consequences of sin in our lives…big or small, committed in secret or in the open…We all must admit that we struggle with the issue of sin. But we do have a choice. Just as Adam and Eve were free to choose God's way or their own way, we too can make moral choices that affect our everyday lives. God has not left us without instructions in making these choices.

and God has shown me that my self-centeredness/self-reliance has hurt you. I have been wrong when…

_____

_____

_____

and I know you could have felt

_____.

Will you forgive me?"

3 "I've been learning some new things in our small group. I've learned that it makes God sad when I make wrong choices. He feels sad because he doesn't want to see you or me hurt. What does that make you feel—when you know he hurts when you make wrong choices, such as…

_____

_____

_____?"

Read chapter 14 of *The Unshakable Truth* book.

THE BIBLICAL PROCESS OF MAKING RIGHT CHOICES

Review: How did your TruthTalk assignment go this week? What was the response?

_____

_____

_____

_____

Do you remember when you first learned to tie your shoes? How old were you? _____ Who taught you?_____ Was it hard to learn?_____

Someone read the following.

> At least two people (the more the merrier) who have shoelaces compete in a contest. Each participant un-tie one shoe. Then shut your eyes and on the count

of three, tie your shoe as quickly as possible. When you have completed your task quickly say, "Done."

Ready…set…go!

Tongue-in-cheek questions for the declared winner:

- Was this a difficult task for you? _____

- What was the most difficult part? _____
  _____
  _____

- As a child, how long did it take you to learn the process of tying your shoes?
  _____
  _____

- How is it that you can now easily tie your shoes even with your eyes closed?
  _____
  _____

The apostle Paul said, "I discipline my body like an athlete, training it to do what it should" (1 Corinthians 9:27). Tying our shoes didn't come automatically—we had to train ourselves or learn a process. Is the same true in being trained to make right choices? _____

Someone read Psalm 25:4-5.

Based on this psalm, do obeying God and walking in his ways come automatically, or are they a process we must be trained in and learn? Why or why not?

_____

_____

_____

_____

OUR GROUP OBJECTIVE

To gain a clearer understanding of the process of making right moral choices and a deeper trust in God's ways.

Have you been taught a process for making right moral choices—a process of walking in God's ways? If so, how? If not, why do you suppose no one taught you a process?

_____

_____

_____

_____

Someone read the following.

> Learning to tie your shoes required a certain process to follow, for example, "First take a shoestring

in each hand. Next cross them and then…" Following each step led to a tied pair of shoes. And over time the repeated steps became automatic— you learned the shoe-tying process. In order to make right moral choices, there is a process to follow. It isn't difficult to describe, but it is a challenge to live out because it goes against our natural, sinful nature that is both pridefully self-reliant and self-centered.

Because we all have been affected by inherited sin, choosing right from wrong does not come naturally, let alone automatically, after we become a Christian. It requires a deliberate process of spiritual discipline to keep God in the center of each moral choice.

The following is called the "4-Cs" process. Practiced, learned, and applied to your life, it will guarantee right moral choices every time. Let's describe the process and then practice it together.

1. Consider the Choice

What are some choices you made today—common, everyday choices that are practically automatic? For example, choice of clothes to wear, what time to get up, and so on?

_____

_____

_____

_____

Someone read the following.

> The above kind of choice requires little time to consider. But when a moral choice is involved we need to stop and consider it. For example, the choice of what color shirt or blouse you wear is amoral. But whether you let an unsuspecting customer pay you too much for an item is a moral issue.

Someone read Genesis 3:1-6.

Eve had a choice to make. If God had not forbidden the first couple to eat a certain fruit, would it have been wrong for her to eat it? Why or why not?

_____

_____

_____

_____

So a moral choice is necessary when _____

_____

_____

_____

When is the best time to consider your choices—before, during, or after a temptation? Why?

_____

_____

_____

_____

Moral choices surround the boundaries that God has defined between right and wrong. And as we encounter those choices we must first pause long enough to recognize we are facing an opportunity for a right or wrong decision. Then we…

||||||||||||||||||||||||||||||||||||||||||||||||||||||||||||||||||||||||||||||||||||||||||||

2. Compare the Choice to God

In the Garden the serpent told Eve she wouldn't die if she ate from the tree of the knowledge of good and evil. (See Genesis 3:4.) Was he correct? Why or why not?

_____

_____

_____

_____

How about the serpent's claim that going against God's command would "make them like God"? (See Genesis 3:5.) Was the serpent correct? Why or why not?

_____

_____

_____

_____

Someone read the following.

> What Eve failed to do, like many of us, was to take God into consideration and compare her attitude and action to him, which would have meant looking at the choice in relation to the commands that emanate from his nature. This, of course, would have required that she believe that God was her absolute standard for right—not herself. When we choose to obey God we in are in effect telling him, "I love you enough to place your desires first in my life. You are the sovereign God, whose character and nature defines what is right for me."

> When we pause to consider our choice and then compare our attitude or action to God's character and commands, it requires a number of changes or adjustments from our natural way of thinking and doing. What attitude adjustment must we make toward God?

_____

_____

_____

What adjusted attitude is required toward God's Word?_____

_____

_____

_____

|||||||||||||||||||||||||||||||||||||||||||||||||||||||||||||||||||||||||||||||||||||||||||||||||||||||||

3. Commit to God's Way

The process of making right choices requires that we first stop and consider if the decision we are facing is a choice between right and wrong. Second, we compare that choice to God and his Word. He becomes the arbiter of right and wrong, and his ways define what he desires for us. Third, we commit to his way. This often requires that we search his Word and listen to his Spirit and the wise counsel of others so we can discern God's loving heart behind his standard. Coming to better understand and experience his heart of love will deepen our commitment to his way (see 2 Corinthians 5:14 and Daniel 1:8).

God's way is always in our best interest, so why do we sometimes struggle to commit to it?

_____

_____

_____

_____

Someone read Galatians 5:16-26.

Committing to God's way is dependent on a number of factors related to how you respond to your sinful nature and to the Holy Spirit.

What is the role of the Holy Spirit in you committing to God's way? (verses 17-18, 22-23, 25)

_____

_____

_____

Are your choices ever completely free of what the sinful nature desires? Why or why not? (verses 17-23)

_____

_____

_____

What is your role in committing to God's way? (verses 16, 22-26)

_____

_____

Our choices are never free from the conflict of the sinful nature. But the Holy Spirit has imparted God's divine nature to us and gives us a desire to please him. We are empowered to live out God's divine nature as the love of Christ constrains, or controls, our choices and our behavior. When we submit to the Holy Spirit, allowing the love of Christ to take control of our life, we are empowered to make godly choices that bear the fruit of his Spirit.

4. Count On God's Protection and Provision

Someone read Deuteronomy 10:12-13 and 11:26-28.

Why does obeying and following in God's ways produce his protection and provision?

_____

_____

_____

_____

Someone read the following.

> God wants us to choose his ways, which are right and in our best interest. Choosing right instead of wrong does not sap all the fun and excitement out of life; on the contrary, it accomplishes our good, because we were created to reflect his likeness and image. When we live godly lives—lives that reflect the character of God—we inevitably experience life as God designed it. And that includes being protected from certain things that would cause us harm and being provided with certain things that would bring us joy.

Living a life of integrity, sexual purity, faithfulness, kindness, forgiving others, and patience, and putting the needs of others

ahead of our own, provides for what kinds of things physically, emotionally, spiritually, psychologically, or relationally?

_____

_____

_____

_____

When we avoid a life of lust and sexual immorality, dishonesty, hatred, resentment, selfish ambition, envy, jealousy, and divisiveness it protects us from what kinds of things physically, emotionally, spiritually, psychologically, or relationally?

_____

_____

_____

_____

Someone read Jeremiah 12:1 and Psalm 37:35.

In the short term, morality isn't always rewarded, and immorality isn't always punished. So how can we say that we can truly count on God's protection and provision when we commit to his way?

_____

_____

_____

_____

When Jesus said, "You will know the truth, and the truth will set

you free" (John 8:32), he spoke not only of freedom *from* things like disease, guilt, disillusionment, and despair, but also of freedom *to* love and be loved, to trust, to enjoy peace and joy. Committing to God's way may mean giving up the pleasures and satisfaction of life for a season but in the end we will be free to enjoy all that God intended us to experience. The apostle Paul said it best when he wrote that anything "we suffer now is nothing compared to the glory [God] will give us later."

|||||||||||||||||||||||||||||||||||||||||||||||||||||||||||||||||||||||||||||||||||||||||||||||||||

Truth Encounter

Someone read Psalm 37:3-6.

This passage summarizes the 4-Cs process. As we commit our ways to the Lord, trust in his loving heart for our good, and live out his standards, he will bring great blessings our way.

Take time to share with the group how part or all of the 4-Cs process has been experienced in your life.

Identify a time when you committed to God's way and he provided you a blessing. What was the situation, and what blessing did you experience?

_____

_____

_____

_____

Identify a time when you committed to God's way and he protected you. What was the situation, and what were you protected from?

_____

_____

_____

_____

TruthTalk—An Assignment of the Week

This week take time with a family member or friend and share the 4-Cs process. Consider saying something like:

1 "In our small group we have been discussing how to make right moral choices. I've learned a 4-step process for making right choices every time. The steps are…

_____

_____

_____

_____."

God and God alone is the arbiter of what is right and what is wrong...Everything moral flows from his innate nature. When Adam, Eve, or anyone else decides that they alone know what is right for them, they are in effect worshipping the god of self. Right, godly choices that bring fulfillment and joy to our lives are those that relationally align with the person and character of a holy, righteous God.

2 "In making the right moral choices in life I've come to trust God's heart for me. I know that if he tells me not to do something, it's because he doesn't want me to experience painful things. He wants to protect me from harm. For instance, I made a choice that brought blessing when _____ _____.

And I made a choice that brought pain when _____ _____ _____ _____."

3 "Do you know how to make right choices every time? One of the things you must think about when you have a choice to make is, What does God want you to do in that situation? And how does his answer show you that he loves you? For example, when I was your age I had a particular choice to make about…

_____
_____

_____

_____."

Read chapter 15 of *The Unshakable Truth* book.

||||||||||||||||||||||||||||||||||||||||||||||||||||||||||||||||||||||||||||||||||||||||||||

Close in Prayer

VICTORY OVER SIN THROUGH RIGHT CHOICE

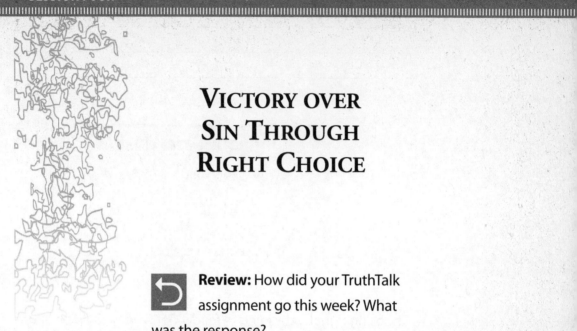

Review: How did your TruthTalk assignment go this week? What was the response?

_____

_____

_____

What Makes Choosing Right Difficult?

Someone read Psalm 15:1-4.

Have you ever had to make a choice you knew was right, but you suffered some type of hurt by doing it? Share that experience with the group.

_____

_____

_____

_____

> ## OUR GROUP OBJECTIVE
>
> To gain a clearer understanding
> of how to keep from rationalizing
> wrong choices and to
> practice the 4-Cs process.

Choosing right by deciding to follow God's way would be easy if it didn't conflict with our wants, needs, or pleasures, as legitimate as some of those may be. Even children, from a young age, struggle to "keep their promises even when it hurts" (Psalm 15:4).

Someone read "Randy's Story" and "Kelly's Story" below. They set up scenarios where the honesty of children—maybe children like yours—is tested.

Randy's Story

My parents had to do some shopping. They told my older sister and me to clean the house while they were gone. As soon as they left, I started watching TV and my sister began cleaning the house. When my parents came home, they said, "Thank you both for making the house so

beautiful. We are going to take both of you out for ice cream for doing all this work." My older sister gave me a mean look, but she did not say anything. I've got a choice to make.

Assuming his sister stays quiet, how does it benefit Randy to say nothing about his failure to follow his parents' instructions to help clean the house?

_____

_____

_____

_____

Assuming Randy speaks up and honestly confesses he didn't help clean the house, what negative consequence is he apt to experience?

_____

_____

_____

_____

So what does Randy do? He reasons that he's done more than his share of work in the past by cleaning up the house when his sister was out playing. So he keeps quiet and enjoys a hot fudge sundae.

Kelly's Story
My friend Amy and I were really thirsty. We both

wanted our own can of a soft drink, but we had
enough money for only one can. I put our money
in the machine. A can came out and, surprisingly,
the money came back too! I am really thirsty and
don't want to share. And now I have enough money
to buy another drink. I've got a choice to make.

What's the benefit of Kelly using the money to buy another soft drink?

_____

_____

_____

_____

What's the negative consequence of turning in the money to the people who run the vending machine?

_____

_____

_____

_____

So what does Kelly do? She reasons that the pop from the machine is overpriced in the first place, so getting two for the price of one is only fair. She buys another soft drink and quenches her thirst.

||||||||||||||||||||||||||||||||||||||||||||||||||||||||||||||||||||||||||||||||||||||||||||||

The Art of Rationalizing

Someone has said that the justification of sin is just as bad as the original sin. Do you agree? Why or why not?

_____

_____

_____

_____

Someone read the following.

> Often, being honest brings short-term pain and be-
> ing dishonest provides a short-term benefit. So in
> those cases, as in the stories of Kelly and Randy
> above, we tend to rationalize and justify our actions.

Be vulnerable and share an example of how seductive rationalizing can be. Have you ever cheated on an exam as a student? How did you justify it through rationalization? Have you ever fudged on your income tax or kept silent when a clerk undercharged you? Have you gone over the speed limit? How did you justify those things? How about changing your score for the better during a game of golf or a friendly game of cards? How did you justify that? Honesty is good for the soul. Share your own art of rationalization with the group.

_____

_____

_____

_____

_____

_____

_____

||||||||||||||||||||||||||||||||||||||||||||||||||||||||||||||||||||||||||||||||||

How to Break the
Rationalization Syndrome

Really, what harm is done by fudging a golf-game score or going over the speed limit or taking a few bogus deductions on your income tax? If no one is really hurt, what harm is there?

_____

_____

_____

_____

When we disobey God's commands, is it just his laws we violate, or do we violate something else also? If something in addition is violated, what is it?

_____

_____

_____

_____

Someone read Psalm 19:7-11.

This passage says the law, decrees, precepts, and commandments of God are perfect, trustworthy, right, clear, pure, true,
and so on. Are these descriptors referring to a set of rules, a person, both, or what? Discuss.

_____

_____

_____

_____

The precepts of God are true, perfect, pure, and right because
they flow out of the very person of God. His ways come out of
the very essence and nature of his being. Violate his ways—his
law—and we violate him.

Second Samuel 11 and 12 tells the story of King David and Bathsheba. We are all no doubt familiar with this story. Identify some
of the commandments of God that David violated.

_____

_____

_____

_____

Someone read 2 Samuel 12:13 and Psalm 51:3-4.

These sins, the violations of God's law, violated Bathsheba and
her husband, Uriah. They violated David's responsibility as king
and violated the children of Israel. Yet David said his sin was

against God. Why? How were his sins of adultery, murder, and misusing his authority a sin against God?

_____

_____

_____

_____

Someone read 2 Samuel 12:7-10.

God was David's provider. God had given David everything he needed, and if he had needed more God would have given him even more. But Scripture said that David despised, "counted worthless," two things. They were _____ and

_____.

So how did David's violation of God's law hurt God personally?

_____

_____

_____

_____

Someone read the following.

> When we rationalize and justify our choices
> to shade the truth, unfairly gain from another,
> become unfaithful to our spouse, allow our sharp
> tongue to hurt another, or selfishly bring heart-
> ache and pain to those we love—we hurt first and

foremost our Savior, Jesus. Imagine that our selfish ambition, impatience, envy, jealousy, or selfish desire for pleasure is declaring to Jesus' face, "I don't trust you anymore to give me what I need when I need it. That is why I must take what I need. I no longer believe you have my best interest at heart. I really count you worthless as my Provider and Protector. You say in your Word that God 'himself gives life and breath to everything and he satisfies every need there is' (Acts 17:25), but I don't believe you satisfy my needs—that's why I have to meet them myself."

Imagine how such rationalization and justification of our disobedience would cut the heart of the One who loves us more than we can know. He gave his very life to redeem us back to him. He wants us to trust him and believe that he knows what is best for us and that he will meet our needs on his timetable, not ours. And our disobedience tells him we despise him—that we count his love and need-meeting ability as worthless.

This is perhaps a long ways from what you really mean when you disobey God's commands. But if you thought that your rationalization might affect his heart that way, how would it give you caution? How would it alter your motivation to follow God's commands when you know your disobedience says to

him, "I don't trust you any longer to be my Provider and Protector"? Comment.

_____

_____

_____

_____

_____

_____

_____

Truth Encounter

Following is a case study that challenges you to live out God's ways.

A Case Study in Showing Mercy: "What Goes Around Comes Around"

Read the following together as a group. Put yourself in this situation and work through the 4-Cs process, realizing your obedience to God's commands actually deepens your intimate relationship with him.

You are a bank loan officer and are doing some grocery shopping on your day off. As you are loading your trunk with groceries in the parking lot, a lady puts a deep scrape in your car with her cart. You speak up and say, "Excuse me, Ma'am, you just put a big scratch in my car with that cart."

"You shouldn't have parked your car so close to the cart return," she replies. "It's your problem, not mine."

"Now wait a minute," you respond. "I want this taken care of. Please give me your insurance information."

"I'm out of here," comes the reply. "My insurance won't cover that." And the woman walks quickly to her car and drives off. In your frustration, you fail to write down her car's license plate number.

What are you feeling toward this woman at this point?

_____

_____

_____

_____

Someone read Ephesians 4:26-27.

An injustice has been done. Is it okay to feel angry? Why or why not?

_____

_____

_____

_____

Continue…

> A week later you are on the job at your bank. You're processing a car-loan application that is on the borderline of qualifying. The bank manager tells you that the approval is your call. The applicant has just come in to determine whether she is approved, and she sits down in front of your desk. To your surprise it is the same woman who put the scratch in your car. However, she doesn't recognize you.

||||||||||||||||||||||||||||||||||||||||||||||||||||||||||||||||||||||||||||||||||

1. Consider the choice

Do you approve the loan? The woman was discourteous and irresponsible in not taking responsibility for the damage she caused to your car. You have a choice to consider—show mercy, forgive her, and approve the loan…or give her a taste of her own medicine. Don't make your choice yet, but what are you inclined to do?

_____

_____

_____

_____

|||||||||||||||||||||||||||||||||||||||||||||||||||||||||||||||||||||||||||||||||||||||||

2. Compare it to God

Someone read Zechariah 7:9.

Mercy is right and a virtue because it comes from the very nature of God. As Micah declared, he is the one who "delight[s] in showing mercy" (Micah 7:18). King David said that God's "mercy endures forever" (Psalm 107:1 NKJV). Paul noted that "God is so rich in mercy" (Ephesians 2:4). Mercy isn't simply something God shows, it is something he *is*—he is by nature merciful.

How has God shown you his mercy in your life?

_____

_____

_____

_____

|||||||||||||||||||||||||||||||||||||||||||||||||||||||||||||||||||||||||||||||||||||||||

3. Commit to God's ways

Here is your dilemma. Showing this woman mercy may be a good thing, but wouldn't you be awarding an irresponsible

person a loan? Her disrespect and disregard for you and your property expose a character flaw that might make her irresponsible in repayment. She doesn't recognize you, so if you deny the loan for the good of the bank there will be no repercussions. And to be honest, wouldn't it feel good to get even—or, to put it in a way that sounds better—get justice?

What do you do?

_____

_____

_____

||||||||||||||||||||||||||||||||||||||||||||||||||||||||||||||||||||||||||||||||||||||||||||||||

4. Count on God's protection and provision

If you chose to not approve the loan, you might not suffer any lost protection or provision from God. But if you did show mercy and grant the loan, you can count on a few things.

Read Luke 6:38.

- By showing mercy you can count on God to protect you from _____.

Read Matthew 6:14.

- Showing mercy provides _____ from God and protects you from God's _____ _____.

It's relatively easy to show mercy to the merciful. But it requires a commitment to God's way to show mercy to the undeserving. Jesus said, "Blessed are the merciful, for they will be shown mercy" (Matthew 5:7 NIV).

TruthTalk—An Assignment of the Week

This week share with a family member or friend how rationalizing affects our moral choices. Consider saying something like:

1 "In my small group we have been talking about why it's not always easy to make right choices. I find I have a tendency to rationalize my wrong choices and behaviors. I am asking God's Spirit to help me be attentive to him, such as his desire for me to…

_____

_____

_____."

2 "In my small group this week we've been discussing how

Trusting in Christ to redeem us does protect us from the permanent consequences of sin (eternal death and separation from God) and provides eternal life with Christ to us and all our loved ones who have equally trusted in Christ. But that eternal salvation will not protect us from the negative consequences of making wrong choices here on earth. As Christians there are guidelines to follow and a process of making godly choices.

making right choices has a lot to do with being sensitive to God's Spirit. And I am asking God to help me be different in my relationship with you too. I've asked him to help me avoid rationalizing my behaviors, such as…

_____

_____

_____

_____ .

I am open to any feedback you might have for me too."

3 "I certainly want to make right choices that please God in my life. I've been learning how important it is not to make excuses for my wrong choices. I've been asking God to help me be more/less…

_____

_____

_____

_____."

Review Chapter 14 of *The Unshakable Truth* book and read page 149.

⁞⁞⁞

Close in Prayer

TEACHING RIGHT CHOICES WITHIN YOUR FAMILY AND COMMUNITY

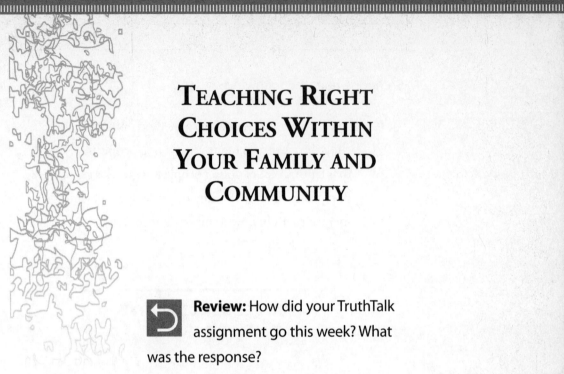

Review: How did your TruthTalk assignment go this week? What was the response?

_____

_____

_____

_____

Someone read Titus 2:6-8.

Based on this passage, what method of teaching young people was Paul instructing his audience to use?

_____

_____

_____

_____

_____

_____

Someone read the following:

> The early church employed a method of modeling the truth and mentoring young people in that truth. A lot of young people today lack a support group of adults willing to model for them and mentor them in how to make right choices.

OUR GROUP OBJECTIVE

To plan a group activity in order to engage in a modeling and mentoring process with some specific young people in your church or community.

In this session you as a group are to brainstorm about an effort to model love and concern to some young people and share what you have learned about making right choices through the 4-Cs process. These young people could be those at risk—meaning those who are fatherless, are from broken homes, or are living in poverty, or who have had run-ins with the law.

One idea would be to interact with some community leaders

and explain how some of your group would like to sponsor a weekend outing, a trip to the zoo, or a time at the park for games…any activity that would give you an opportunity to share some time and love with these kids.

Teach the 4-Cs process to the community leaders before the activity takes place. During your outing, ask the community leaders to re-teach the 4-Cs process to the young people. This will maximize their receptivity and openness to the content. Be prepared as a group to share how important making right choices is for all of us and specific examples of how this process has been relevant and helpful in your own life. Make a priority of establishing ongoing relationships with the young people you meet. Don't let this be a one-time event.

Brainstorm: _____

_____

_____

_____

_____

_____

_____

Take the time here to plan your project using the steps below:

Identify your activity: _____

_____

_____

_____

Set the date and time for your activity: _____

_____

_____

_____

Determine what is needed to execute your activity: _____

_____

_____

_____

Assign responsibilities and tasks. Who will be doing what? _____

_____

_____

_____

Have someone in your group track and record what is being done. This is to record the results of your efforts.

_____

_____

_____

Bring every aspect of your activity before the Lord.

Someone read Titus 2:11-14.

What should we as God's people be doing while we look forward to Christ's return?

_____

_____

_____

_____

Assignment of the Week

Execute your activity.

Close in Prayer

Take the Complete Unshakable Truth® Journey!

The Unshakable Truth Journey gets to the heart of what being a true follower of Christ means and what knowing him is all about. Each five-session course is based one of 12 core truths of the Christian faith presented in Josh and Sean McDowell's book *The Unshakable Truth*®.

The Unshakable Truth Journey is uniquely positioned for today's culture because it 1) highlights how Christianity's beliefs affect relationships, 2) promotes a relational, group context in which Christians can experience the teaching in depth, and 3) shows believers how they can live out Christianity's central truths before their community and world.

More than just a program, The Unshakable Truth Journey is a tool for long-term change and transformation!

CREATED—EXPERIENCE YOUR UNIQUE PURPOSE is devoted to the truth that God is—he exists, and he created human beings for a reason. It lays a foundation for who people are because they're God's creation, who God designed them to be, and how they can live a life of fulfillment.

INSPIRED—EXPERIENCE THE POWER OF GOD'S WORD explores the truth that God has spoken and revealed himself to humanity within the Bible. Further, he gave us his Word for a very clear purpose—to provide for us and protect us.

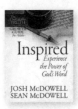

BROKEN—EXPERIENCE VICTORY OVER SIN examines the truth about humankind's brokenness because of original sin, humankind's ongoing problem with sin, and how instead to make right choices in life.

ACCEPTED—EXPERIENCE GOD'S UNCONDITIONAL LOVE opens up the truth about God's redemption plan. The truth that God became human establishes his unconditional acceptance of us, which defines our worth. God values us in spite of our sin. This is the basis on which we gain a high sense of worth.

SACRIFICE—EXPERIENCE A DEEPER WAY TO LOVE digs into the truth about Christ's atonement. The truth that Christ had to die to purchase our salvation shows the true meaning of love—and how God can bring us into a right relationship with him in spite of our sin.

FORGIVEN—EXPERIENCE THE SURPRISING GRACE OF GOD explores the truth about the power of God's grace. The truth that God can offer us forgiveness in spite of our sin helps us understand how we actually obtain a relationship with him.

GROWING—EXPERIENCE THE DYNAMIC PATH TO TRANSFORMATION speaks to the truth about our transformed life in Christ. The truth about our transformed life in Christ defines who we are in this world and shows how we can know our purpose in life.

RESURRECTED—EXPERIENCE FREEDOM FROM THE FEAR OF DEATH focuses on the truth about Christ's resurrection. The truth that Christ rose from the grave and that his resurrection is a historical event assures us of eternal life and overcomes any fear of dying.

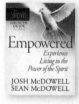

EMPOWERED—EXPERIENCE LIVING IN THE POWER OF THE SPIRIT covers the truth about the Trinity. The truth that God is three in one and defines how relationships work through the Holy Spirit lays the foundation for how we can experience the power of the Spirit.

PERSPECTIVE—EXPERIENCE THE WORLD THROUGH GOD'S EYES examines the truth about God's kingdom and how it defines a biblical worldview. These sessions show how to gain a biblical worldview.

COMMUNITY—EXPERIENCE JESUS ALIVE IN HIS PEOPLE opens up the truth about the church. The truth about Christ's body—the church—provides us with our mission in life and shows us how to experience true community.

RESTORED—EXPERIENCE THE JOY OF YOUR DESTINY is devoted to the truth about the return of Christ. The truth that Jesus is coming back helps us grasp our destiny in life and gain an eternal perspective on life and death.

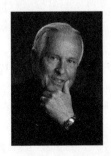

Cover by Koechel Peterson & Associates, Inc., Minneapolis, Minnesota

BROKEN—EXPERIENCE VICTORY OVER SIN
Course 3 of The Unshakable Truth® Journey Growth Guides
Copyright © 2011 by Josh McDowell Ministry and Sean McDowell
Published by Harvest House Publishers
Eugene, Oregon 97402
www.harvesthousepublishers.com

ISBN 978-0-7369-4641-4

Printed in the United States of America

11 12 13 14 15 16 17 18 19 / VP-SK / 10 9 8 7 6 5 4 3 2 1

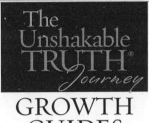

The Unshakable TRUTH® Journey

GROWTH GUIDES
for Adults

D1607274

Broken

Experience
Victory over Sin

JOSH McDOWELL
SEAN McDOWELL

HARVEST HOUSE PUBLISHERS

EUGENE, OREGON